D0310162

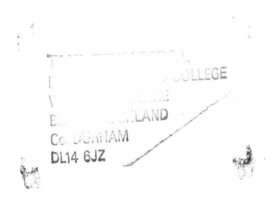

# I am a _____
# PENTECOSTAL

**Brenda Pettenuzzo**
meets
**Josephine Regis**

**Photography: Chris Fairclough**

Religious Consultant: Pastor Io Smith

**FRANKLIN WATTS**

LONDON/NEW YORK/SYDNEY/TORONTO

Josephine Regis is eleven years old.
She lives with her family in
Walthamstow, London. Her father,
John, is a carpenter by trade, and her
mother, Jenny, is a field worker for
the Zebra project, which aims to make
and strengthen links between black
and white Christians. Josephine has
three sisters and one brother.

# Contents

© 1986 Franklin Watts   12a Golden Square   London W1

ISBN 0 86313 428 9

Design: Edward Kinsey
Illustrations: Tony Payne
Cover Design: Steve Wilson

Printed in Italy

The publishers would like to thank the Regis family and the Congregation of the New Testament Assembly, Leyton in East London for their help in the preparation of this book. Special thanks are due to Pastor Smith and Pastor Bailey.

Brenda Pettenuzzo is a teacher of Science and Religion at St Angela's Ursuline Convent School, a Comprehensive School in the London borough of Newham.

Pastor Io Smith is the General Secretary of the New Testament Assemblies, United Kingdom.

## The Pentecostal belief

**The Pentecostal Church is a Christian church. We are followers of Jesus Christ.**

Members of the Pentecostal Churches believe firmly in the Bible, and always try to live their lives by it. They believe that Jesus Christ is the Son of God and He was put to death to pay the price for all the wrong things that people do. They believe that He rose from the dead and will return to earth to establish His Kingdom.

## I have been coming to our Church since I was small, but I wasn't "born" a Pentecostal!

Nobody is a "born" Pentecostal, because to become one, a person has to be converted. That means that they have realised that Jesus died for them, and have promised to start a new way of life. Many Pentecostals were members of other Christian churches first. They were converted and joined the Pentecostal church. Some people still attend a more traditional Christian church and a Pentecostal church.

## Our Church

**There are many types of Pentecostal churches. Our Church is called the New Testament Assembly.**

Most Pentecostal churches are not very old. Some started in Great Britain, some in the United States or the West Indies. The New Testament Assembly church started in Jamaica about thirty years ago. Josephine and her family go to the church in Leyton.

**Our leader is called Pastor Smith. As well as leading the worship at our church she does many other things.**

The members of the Pentecostal Churches are called "sister" or "brother" or, for the older women, "mother". This is because they feel close to one another as members of God's family. Their Pastor is like a shepherd and looks after the "flock" or congregation. Pastors can be men or women and at Josephine's church the Pastor is a woman, Pastor Io Smith. Many of her congregation call on her for help and advice.

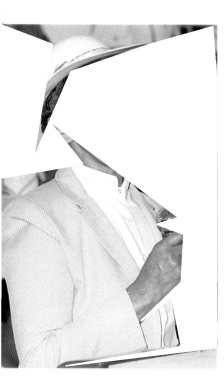

## On Sundays

**We have two main services at our Church on Sundays, and most people go to both of them.**

Josephine and her family always go to the Divine Worship Service which lasts from midday until about half past two. Pastor Bailey, the assistant Pastor, usually begins the service with a prayer and a Bible reading. Pastor Smith then leads the congregation in prayer and in their praising of God.

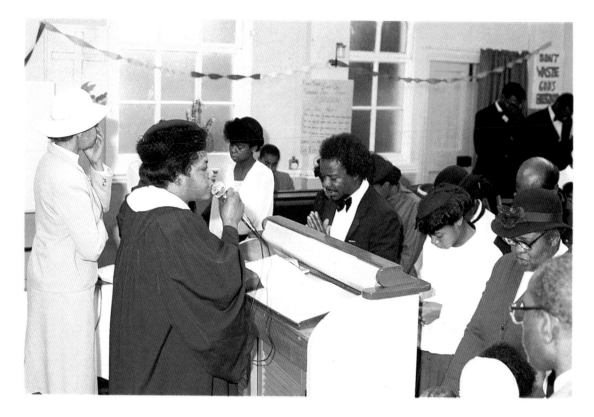

**Sometimes my Dad reads from the Bible at church. He also studies at home and goes out to Bible study on Monday evenings.**

Bible study is very important to Pentecostals. Each Sunday the service includes a sermon based on a part of the Bible. Sometimes the sermon is preached by Pastor Smith and sometimes by visiting Pastors. Many people feel very moved by what is said and they call out in agreement. Outside the Church, passers-by can hear the congregation praising the Lord!

## My mum and dad and my older sisters sing in the choir.

Music is very important in all Pentecostal Churches. At Josephine's church there is a choir which sings at every service. There are men and women in the choir, and an organist. Sometimes there are other instruments, and there are always tambourines. The Choir leads the congregation when it is singing. Their voices are always very impressive, even when only a few people are in the Church.

**It is hard to stand still while we are singing. Everyone joins in and claps their hands.**

The choir often goes to sing at other churches, and other choirs come to sing at Josephine's church. The standard of singing is very high. Pentecostal Churches are well known for their singing, and visitors to Josephine's church very quickly feel the urge to join in. The congregation worships in music and prayer. Sometimes the same chorus is repeated over and over again, but everyone knows when to stop!

## The Lord's Supper

**We have another service at our Church on Sunday evening and once a month we celebrate the Lord's Supper.**

On the last Sunday of every month the congregation of the New Testament Assembly remembers the last meal which Jesus shared with His followers before His death. It starts with prayer and singing. There is a sermon from the Pastor, and time for private prayer. There may also be a healing service, then the Breaking of Bread service begins.

**Pastor Smith does what Jesus did at the Last Supper, and we all share the bread and wine.**

Pastor Smith says a blessing over the bread and wine, and repeats the words of Jesus. At the Last Supper, He said that the bread and wine were His body and blood. Church elders take the bread and wine to the congregation. As they eat and drink, the people are remembering that Jesus did this before He died for everyone's sins.

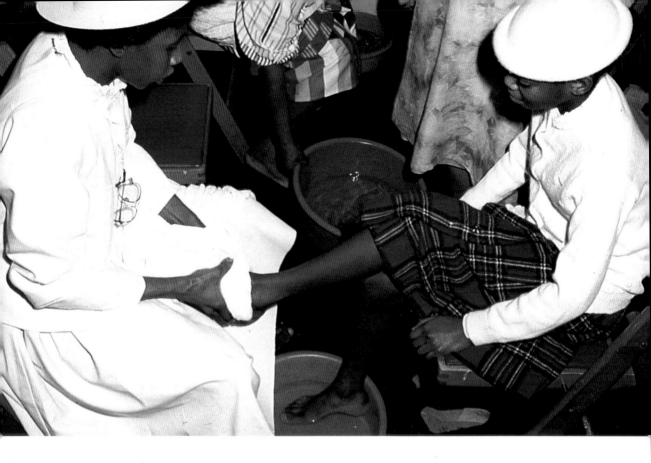

## Washing the feet

**After the Lord's Supper, we wash one another's feet. We have to choose someone that we don't know very well!**

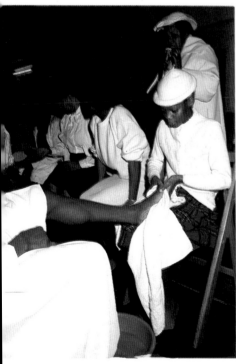

At the Last Supper, Jesus washed the feet of His Disciples. They didn't want Him to do it, because they thought He was so much greater than them. He told them that He was setting them an example of how to behave. The congregation sit down in pairs and washes one another's feet.

# Healing

**We often have a healing service on Sundays.**

Healing takes place in many Pentecostal churches. It often forms part of one of the regular services. While the whole congregation is praying for them, people come up to the platform. The Pastor puts her hands on each one and everyone prays for them to be healed. Sometimes people find that their problem has gone away, and everyone finds it a very moving experience.

# The history of Josephine's family

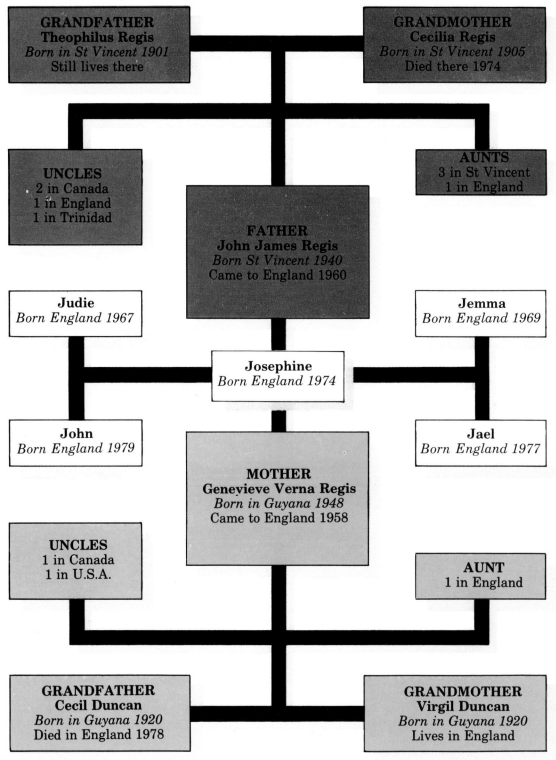

**GRANDFATHER**
Theophilus Regis
*Born in St Vincent 1901*
Still lives there

**GRANDMOTHER**
Cecilia Regis
*Born in St Vincent 1905*
Died there 1974

**UNCLES**
2 in Canada
1 in England
1 in Trinidad

**AUNTS**
3 in St Vincent
1 in England

**FATHER**
John James Regis
*Born St Vincent 1940*
Came to England 1960

**Judie**
*Born England 1967*

**Jemma**
*Born England 1969*

**Josephine**
*Born England 1974*

**John**
*Born England 1979*

**Jael**
*Born England 1977*

**MOTHER**
Genevieve Verna Regis
*Born in Guyana 1948*
Came to England 1958

**UNCLES**
1 in Canada
1 in U.S.A.

**AUNT**
1 in England

**GRANDFATHER**
Cecil Duncan
*Born in Guyana 1920*
Died in England 1978

**GRANDMOTHER**
Virgil Duncan
*Born in Guyana 1920*
Lives in England

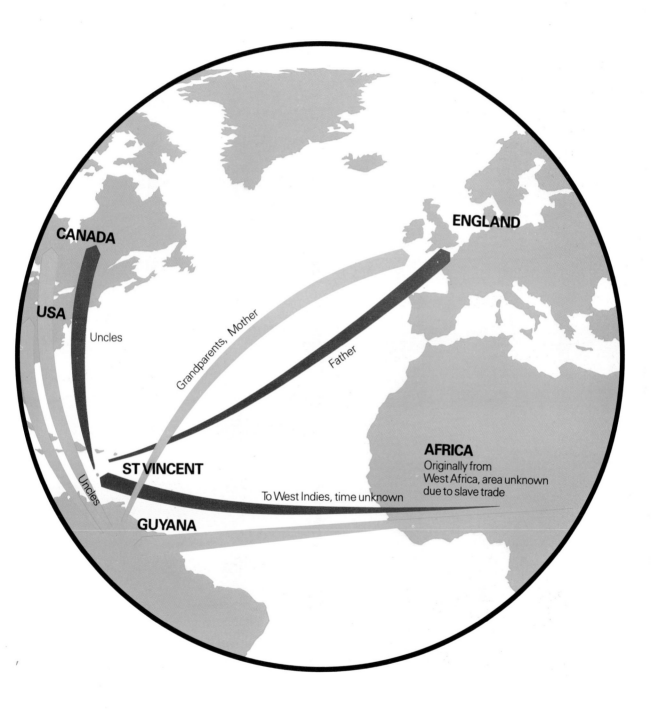

## Sunday School

**On Sunday mornings we all go to our Church for Sunday School.**

From 10.30 am to midday on Sundays, before the Divine Worship service, many of the children from the congregation of the New Testament Assembly gather for Sunday School. They are divided into three groups, according to their ages. Most weeks they have a verse from Scripture to be learned by heart. This is called a Golden Text, and each child recites their's to the whole class.

**Sunday School is a bit like ordinary school, we have homework to do!**

The children each have an exercise book for their work and their homework. As well as the Sunday activities they have special programmes at Christmas and Easter. Sometimes they celebrate a special event by reciting poems or scripture, and by singing hymns for one another. In the Summer there is a Vacation Bible School which lasts for four weeks in the school holidays.

## Baptism

**I was baptised last year because I wanted to become a full member of our Church.**

Some Christian Churches believe that it is best to join their church and be baptised as babies. In the Pentecostal Church baptism is a sign that a person has decided to accept Jesus Christ as their Saviour. Only someone grown up can decide this, so in the Pentecostal church people usually wait until they are grown up before they are baptised.

**At my baptism I had to go into the water and it went right over my head.**

Josephine was quite young to be baptised, but her parents and the Pastor had talked to her about it beforehand. They knew that she was old enough to understand. In the Pentecostal Church, baptism means being completely immersed in water. Jesus was baptised in this way in the River Jordan. This is an outward symbol that a work of conversion has taken place inside that person's heart.

# Getting married

**Couples who are going to get married have their engagement blessed first.**

The two people who intend to get married come along to one of the Sunday services. The Pastor calls the couple out to the front of the Church and talks to them and to the rest of the congregation on the subject of Marriage. Then she blesses the couple, their engagement, and their engagement rings.

**After a few months the couple have their marriage blessed in the Church.**

The congregation is always very happy when two of their members get married. The whole Church celebrates. Lots of people meet and marry through being members of our Church. Many of the older generation of Church members were married in other Churches. The younger people who have grown up as members of the New Testament Assembly come to their Church to prepare for marriage.

## At home

**My mum cooks lovely dinners for us all. We always say grace before meals at home.**

Josephine's mother cooks many dishes which come from the Caribbean. The family usually manages to have its evening meal together even though they are often busy doing Church activities in the evenings. They take it in turns to say a prayer before the meal. The prayer is both a blessing and a thanksgiving for the food they are about to eat.

**We have lots of books at home. My Mum and Dad read them with us and help us to learn more about our Faith.**

Josephine's parents are both keen to help their children understand the Bible. They have many books with stories from the Old and New Testaments of the Bible. Josephine and her brother and sisters also pray before they go to sleep at night. They thank God for the good things which happen and pray for their friends and relatives.

# The Pentecostal Year

The Pentecostal year, like that of all the other Christian Churches, is based upon the normal calendar year. Pentecostals do not single out Saints and other special people for individual attention. They pay most respect to the Festivals of Christmas and Easter, and they have certain other special events during the year.

**CHRISTMAS**
*December 25th*
The celebration of the
birth of Jesus Christ.

**NEW**
**ASSE**
**LEYTON**
*November*
A special servic
to which local
dignitaries are in
e.g. Police Chief, M
Mayor.

**VACATION BIBLE
SCHOOL**
*August*
An annual trip for young
people.

## NATIONAL YOUTH CONFERENCE
*February*
For young members of New Testament Assembly Churches all over Britain. Held at a different venue each year.

## PREPARATION FOR THE ANNUAL CONVENTION
*March/April*
Six weeks of prayer and fasting to prepare for the annual Convention held at Easter.

## EASTER WEEK
*April/May*
This includes Good Friday when Jesus was crucified, and Easter Sunday when Jesus rose from the dead.

# Facts and figures

The Pentecostal movement is part of the Christian Church. It is quite young. It grew out of a revival movement which took place in many parts of the world at the same time, at the beginning of the twentieth century.

Pentecostalists believe in living their lives as the early Christians did. They use the Bible as their guide and they base their belief on the life of Jesus Christ as recorded in the Gospel of Luke.

There are many branches of the Pentecostal movement in Britain today. Some are very small groups which meet in private homes, some are very big congregations which meet in large halls. Many have built their own churches, or bought them from other Christian groups which no longer use them. Unlike many other Christian churches, the Pentecostal churches are growing in number.

The New Testament Assembly is one of the Black Pentecostal Churches which began to grow in Britain after 1950, when many people from the West Indies came to this country. It was founded in Jamaica in the early nineteen-fifties, and came to Britain in 1960. There are nineteen branches of the church in Britain, and the headquarters is at the church in Tooting, south west London. Each church has a Pastor as well as church elders or Deacons, teachers and evangelists to help in the work of the Church. At the headquarters there is an overseer, Bishop Powell, and his assistant, to look after all 19 New Testament Assemblies.

There are many other types of Pentecostal Churches, and there are small differences between them, but they all have certain things in common. They believe that the Bible is the Word of God, that it is true, and is the authority on how to act in every situation. Membership of the Churches is always through a Baptism involving immersion in water, and after an experience of conversion. Babies are not Baptised, only those persons old enough to know what conversion means. Many Pentecostals experience "Baptism in the Spirit" which means being filled with the Holy Spirit and speaking in "Tongues" – speech which has to be understood through an interpreter.

# Glossary

**Bible** The Sacred writings of Christianity, divided into Old and New Testaments. The Old Testament contains books dating back to ancient Jewish times. The New Testament contains the Life and Teachings of Jesus Christ and the preaching of His followers to the early Church.

**Conversion** This is the word used to describe what happens when a person decides to become a Christian. They give up their old way of life and try to live in the way that Jesus Christ expects. When a Pentecostal experiences Conversion, a great change takes place in their life and they receive an inner strength which helps them live a better life.

**Crucifixion** The manner in which Jesus was put to death. It means being fixed to a cross of wood by means of nails or ropes, and left to die from suffocation. It was a very painful death.

**Deacon** A senior member of the congregation who helps in the running of the church, sitting on the management committee and being of practical help to the Pastor.

**Disciples** These were the early followers of Jesus, many of whom went out after He left the earth to pass on His teachings to other parts of the world.

**Evangelist** In the early Christian church the Evangelists were the writers of the Gospels. These are the four books from which we learn about Christ's life. In the modern Pentecostal church Evangelists are Lay Preachers. They are not ordained as Pastors, but they assist the Pastors by preaching at services. Sometimes if the Pastor is going to be delayed, the Evangelist might start the service instead.

**Last supper** Jesus was crucified on Good Friday at the beginning of an important Jewish festival, the Passover. To celebrate this it was usual to have a special meal with one's friends. Jesus did this on the day before, Thursday, and that special meal, the last one with His friends, is called the Last Supper.

**Overseer** A leading Pastor. In the New Testament Assembly the Overseer looks after all the branches of the Church in the United Kingdom.

**Pastor** An ordained Minister of the Pentecostal Church. The Pastor's role is to teach the congregation, pray with them, and care for them, often in a very practical way.

# Index